Resurrected Body

Resurrected Body

poems by

Elizabeth C. Garcia

Cider Press Review
San Diego

Cider Press Review
PO BOX 33384
San Diego, CA, USA
ciderpressreview.com

First edition
10 9 8 7 6 5 4 3 2 1 0

ISBN: 9781930781658
Library of Congress Control Number: 2024940702

Cover photo "Day 23, 'What Was and What Will Be'" courtesy
Graham Francoise.
Author photograph by Rommel Garcia
Book design by Caron Andregg

Winner of the 2023 *Cider Press Review* Editors' Prize Book Award:
ciderpressreview.com/bookaward.

Printed in the United States of America
at Bookmobile in Minneapolis, MN USA.

for my daughters

Shall I be raised from death, the spirit asks.
And the sun says yes.
And the desert answers
your voice is sand scattered in wind.

—Louise Glück

Contents

derrick

What to Expect When You're Expecting

You will be spatchcocked
your sternum, your backbone scissored out
you will be parts without sum
two dead legs like sturgeon
and one pulsing muscle
the last secrets of your body
splayed on the table like a butcher's shop
where all the open wounds of your life are for sale
and you will do as you're told
and you'll still fight it
your voice weak, half-hearted
stop looking, move away
and when they hold it up
you will not recognize this thing
fists tight against its face
waiting for the next right hook

karst

"I knew, and could distinguish nothing."

—Mary Shelley, *Frankenstein*

Motherhood as Safety Coffin

—for Emily Cook Dyches

No one told me love could be
a slow suffocation, a silence

not bird-flecked or tree-hushed,
but mute as tuber, a mothless dark

with nothing bright to howl at.
Here I bear every imaginable load,

loam the only revelation,
fossil only bone, the stories

only for the living.
There was no death test

that I recall—no tarsal-sawing,
no smoke blown enema,

no invisible-inked note
perched on my nose to read

You are really dead—I guess
because I never asked for one?

Have I yessed myself here,
(is this confessable?) believing

I am the bulb birther, the crocus coach?
I coax the tulip to unfurl like a plume and push.

Houdini, I heard, once clawed his way
through the chert, his body arrowed

upward, arriving like a winged onion,
like spring itself, panicked and gasping.

Is there any hunger for the young
other than being seen?

Could you string my fingers to a bell
to loosen its tongue, to lick the night

with ululation, would there be any keeper there
with ears to hear it?

Self-portrait as Sinkhole I

Here is the sequence: H_2O
        (what too much drowns us) plus CO_2 (what burns
                the drowning) breeds

carbonate (carbon eaten)
        something to gnaw on earth bones.

But if loss like a sinkhole
        is the birth of a void
                which buoys up to the surface,

it must, then, be there before we buckle,
        before Jeffrey Bush, age 37, and his whole bedroom

collapse into one brief gasp of the earth,
        his yellow hat still racked on the doorknob,

before the cops wrestle his brother from the pile,
        straddling the jagged slabs, the mattress
                still pinking from the dirt like a blossom.

When they demolish the house, the ground still doubtful, shifty,
        he digs offerings from the rubble:
                some medals, a picture of mom,

a Bible. Everyone points: *There, that's God*
        so Jeremy clutches Him, dusty, to his chest

and two years later (or before?)
        when the hole, still hungry
                gulps down the mound of white rock

(closest they could come to hallowing)
        he's there to see it because he never left,

lives two blocks away, and every day walks back
        to the fenced-off site, a circle in a square, a token
            saying *there, there.*

Every day the slow acid drip,
        trying to rip the meaning off things like a price tag—
            it wasn't God, just crumbling rock—

listing what else he could have done:
        swallow sand—disappear—
            dig for his brother's hand

so he wouldn't be alone?
    Do we always get wrong when to let go?

Somewhere in this pile

of plastic wrap, stacks of yellow bowls,
blue-lidded pyrex, the metal-slick clink of gifts

we hope will last for years and several children,
is the woman you married, the girl you loved

before she became Woman of the House, Your
House, the garage too crowded

for two cars. Her arm stretches across your bed like Iowa
before she touches flesh. And you reach out

with closed eyes, hold her bone warmth, not knowing
she is still outside, trying to think of words

to name it all. Remembering: it was Adam
who got the naming power, made Eve

Mother before she could be Girl. How long
did it take for her to turn

toward that sound? Did she sense the girl
inside, the muted memory, the leaves

in her periphery, twitching? Or just
hunger, a stomach growling

for self—a woman with all things given to her
who wanted. And when she eats the fruit,

she'll devour the Memory in its flesh—
her elusive Daughter-ness—

suck Her story from its pit,
lick clean her sticky palms,

her living fingertips, stretch them out behind her
to touch a Father's hand.

Dad Feels Like Daniel Boone Inside

I discover this in the ER, his shirt opened up
to EKG sensors, to skin I haven't seen in years,

all the hair a white I remember: grandpa,
naked at the bathroom door, *Doris! Turn off that dishwasher!*

not knowing I was sitting there with my pudding pop
watching the soaps.

We've been here for an hour now, my mother
answering the nurse for him, and hovering,

so he gives up. Makes the radiology tech tilt his bed to the TV
so he can find something cowboy-looking, the colors muted—

a prairie woman with a bouffant 'do and blue eye shadow.
The colored lines of the monitors all undulate—

all but one, flat and blue. I joke to Mom: *Is that for brain activity?*
She grins, and he's oblivious, intent on how the drunk

will finish chopping all that wood: Boone's justice,
meted out for some sin I've missed in the plot,

the volume pointed only at him—though I could make up
some offense in black and white put right, the squabble

of some village where gunslingers flick out clichés
with nimble wrists, tipping hats to ladies who sashay through town

and bonnet back their words, who clang with suppertime,
scratching out their lives with washboard knuckles. The place

where Boone's voice resonates through the woods,
deep and mellow, the mountain lion and the lamb

warm their hands to its amber glow,
and my father's heart returns to sinus rhythm.

At the Bottom of Moreton Bay

1.

at the bottom of Moreton Bay
are ships younger than I,
rusting

to be precise:
thirty-six steel pontoons
loads of concrete pipes, of cars

the Lady Norman
Estrella del Mar
and one fifty-meter coal barge

giants scabbed over with barnacles,
sulking on the bottom
like Job covered in pink boils

and among their scaly hulks swim
blue gropers
giant yellow-streaked trevally

banded wobbegongs
shuffling through the sand
like sock puppets

2.

to raise
a two-thousand-year-old Roman ship
from the Rhone

they cut it
into three pieces
to hoist into the quay

what is the calculus
to lift the body
to will it another atomic mass

3.

in Antikythera, they pulleyed up
marbled Hercules, Ulysses,

copies of heroes, the crane groaning

i am the marble
and the machinery

4.

last year
a woman's baby died

she put it
in a concrete block

the block she put
in a tote bag

what is the tensile strength
of my heart

5.

putting babies to bed
the minutes
are slow as history

two hundred   years of oak
a bulk of   mastodon
fossils long   buried, long

sanded and ashed,
their grit   a new kind
of gravity

how long will this last?
how do I answer
after two, are you done?

Motherhood is not unlike Philippe Petit

walking the tightrope between Notre Dame's two towers
gripping the long pole, every muscle tensed to survival,
to the mantra you recite in your head:

> *don't look down,*
> *don't look down,*
> *don't look—*

and in the cathedral below, the priests
have convened in their polyester vestments,
their bodies housed in their chasubles, decked

in pectoral crosses, dalmatics and cassocks,
belted and mitered, cinctured with stoles and tassels
their copes, their multi-syllabics of cloth

they're reading their mandates from the Holy See
they're laying on the heads of other men their hands
they're singing in the name of Christ and every holy saint

> *Bless these chosen men*
> *Bless and sanctify these chosen men*
> *Bless, sanctify, and consecrate these chosen men*

When she wakes, rigid

stroke her hair, and rock.
Open the curtain, watch the flashing,
the light's bright amnesia, the careening trees,
that suffocation, apocalypse, another plummet
down the stairs into another
tunnel, another muscled abandonment,
bursting into the world again,
her fists tight against her face.

And when you say,
That's thunder
It's a loud noise

believe the world is not so scary when it's named.
Believe that she is armed now
against that vertigo
and she won't need you, looking down
at her own child's eyes, black with fear,
her mother's body in a box,
her own incapable hands.

Shit Mom

leaves her boy in the road with his trike, crying
she pushes a stroller drags a vine
she wants to keep its honeysuckle sun
bring the whole field back inside

leaves him alone at home
(sister's late for school) refusing
the shoes, her belly takes a storm
of kicks, a vortex of screams

leaves him with the keys the september car
needs to eat something now—a sandwich yes
just this grocery store

deserves the blue lights *recite—*
backwards!—the alphabet holding
cell jailhouse pasta mug shot, merits
worse than probation scrubbing toilets

deserves the flock of sharp-winged women
their stormswift their *I-would-nevers*
clawing her to eternal torment

does not deserve the grocer listening
as she eats   in slow bites keeping
back the nausea   thinking back

to the open door,   to standing
there   not knowing what to do
in the parking lot   sinking
not knowing what to do

self-portrait as ghost

the way a shoe once was a calf,
    a daughter now dry
        a figless fig

a backyard ball now mossy
    is some residue of red
        I too reside like

a lozenge
    on the tongue
        or up the bum

rags   reeking
    of mildew await their taste
        of vinegar

memory of milk
    left in the hooks
        on a cat's tongue

pay attention
    I have been here
        look

the cabinet doors
    have opened
        with volition

the chairs have moved,
      made room for the broom
            collecting crumbs

dishes, once Sisyphean
      have disappeared
            like green from autumn

here is some purgatory
      kitchen
            and not kitchen

dresses congregate
      in drawers, comparing
            melon stains

language of sustenance
      of subtraction
            so

if your loved objects
      are abducted
            if the lights flicker

if you hear a clatter
      unsourced, some glass
            crashes and breaks

feel some footstep
      not your own,
            some turbulence of the air

some sibilant wind, know
    revenge
            is its own discipline

a hoarded patience
        bright as a scoured pot
                hovering in the air

Looking for the Soul Bone

The Torah says
it's the piece of you
that's indestructible.

Put it in fire,
it won't burn.
Drop an anvil on it,

it will fulcrum underneath,
tip the block
like a wobbly table.

This is the piece I'd like to find,
hold in my hand, examine
its shape, its calcified pores,

the color of scrolls, where I can read
of the salt I came from,
the simple orbit of atoms—

then pocket it for later,
until somewhere
in the woods, I find

the right body of water
to skip it across, listen
to the chord it strums.

Self-portrait as Sinkhole II

If you could name it:
limestone,
dolomite.

If you could witness that first
sulfurous drop,
could calculate

just how little acid water needs
to carve its runnels
into memory like lace,

could you then draft
a theory of subtraction:
if the quotient is disappearance,

how do you isolate
the inner flaw
the infirmity, deduce the value

of a firmament that any moment
could swallow you
in its giant leafy mouth?

You are torturing the page
for that equation, the blackboard
clouded by chalky smears

where x once was, knowing
this will always end in a forest,
in that dream of your father walking away

and you called his name
and he kept walking
your voice clawing the dark

from the air like charcoal, the air
blackening he kept walking
and you who were not the child self

were falling your mouth wide open
face down your mouth filling with dirt
and dead leaves—you

are the mouth. You
are the swallowing,
becoming it.

charnel

"Soon a gentle light stole over the heavens, and gave me a sensation of pleasure. I started up and beheld a radiant form rise from among the trees."

—Mary Shelley, *Frankenstein*

Watermelon, in Sapphics

From a dusty shoe box, I unearth photos,
one a church picnic: my mother feeds my father
watermelon, reaching to him her white arms,
rind in his buried

face, his thirsty audible slurp devouring
flesh. She smiles to see him immersed in melon,
pink of all things female, forgetting all but
contest: to beat your

chest, to beat the others, then let your whiskers
drip with juice, black seeds in your teeth, defeated.
Anyone can change over time, I know. But
this was my father,

green before he ripened, became with age, sweet—
sweeter, putting terms in their place. I savor
such a moment, roll on my tongue the time he
ate from her fingers.

Event Horizon

Age four   maybe five   you open your mother's   jewelry box

to star-fire   dispersion, the strange mechanics   of lobster claws,

chain clasps   bracelets   broken-jawed, ropes   of amber and jade,

heavy fruit of gems, of grandmothers you never knew, bulky shanks

of pewter, of silver pinked like the sky at dusk—

all the ways light can be caught and kept—finds

a pouch   black velvet, finger-sized,   opens it   (*don't*),
inside it a star, a crumb of light, the lowest common denominator
between you and the universe, you are less small, less lost in a house
of voices large as brass bedrails, as broken pianos, you forget it might
slip through your fingers to the rug, colored *old boxes,*
dusty attic, she finds you, drags the shag, rasps her palms
combing for that stone, sobbing, her emblem
of infinity lost to infinity, pulls you both
into a denser, blacker place where
she is no longer your mother
just a woman
wrecked

Leaving California, 1972

She bundled up her baby, all her mother things, her books,
till the blue wagon was full. Her husband drove the whole way,

so she watched the desert, how it stood still for minutes
at a time, only moved when she wasn't looking, like her life,

plucked,   because he had a dream:
they would live in Georgia, where she knew no one,

always thought of race riots and burnings. She only knew
the bite of snow, its burial, freezing eyelash to shard.

And hills over ocean, how fog soothes the spike of city,
blurs the tops of bridges, so you learn to imagine half of everything,

and how it ends. This would keep her looking forward,
watching the green deepen slowly through Texas, cling to her throat

in Louisiana, where she rolled the windows down, clenched her jaw
against the stammer of potholes. Kept her leaning forward

to each town, each traffic light. She didn't know how far apart
they could be, how much could be forgotten between each one,

like the lightning they had raced through Kansas, the calligraphy
of roofs along the road, the snap of trees, like his pocketful

of toothpicks.

Ad for Salems, 1978

—for Mary Reno

Here is a little greenhouse,
   pilgrim. Breathe in
      peppermint, winter.

   Take a break from the babies.
Breathe out the cinders
   of your daughter's house

from the pyres burning there
   the *we-can't-have-that-here*
      in her husband's eyes.

     When your incense of flint and forge
   follows you into the house,
coils down the hall,
   leaves its skin in his boot,
     a milky threat,

   when it scrolls round corners
like a prayer
   its ghost body testifying
     someone has sinned,

   when he says *we have rules*
and means *higher ways—*

   breathe in and out
     until the airport parting,
the gravelly goodbye.

Then, o pilgrim,   then you can plant
     one smoky smack on his lips,
        one kiss like a coal

        on his livid mouth.

Ode to That Truck Driver Who Saved Me in 1978

You probably had things
on your mind. Like Waylon Jennings.
Making it to Dothan
before dark. Your wife you hadn't
made love to, at least
two months. And fields rolling past
your window, yellow land
you wanted to roll in with her. And
a house, sagging in
the trees, a dirty white. Then:
red flutter, highway's
edge. Right foot off the gas,
(a reflex after rodents,
deer) and passing, second glance:

blonde pigtails, red
jumper, baby squat. You eyed
mirrors, hit the brakes,
then, hard, skidded rocks
to stop. And nothing either
way for miles of twilight glimmer.
Flicked your hazards. Climbing
down, you scanned the yard, gleaming
windows, walking stiff,
from aching muscles, nice and slow, if
someone noticed you.
And she was watching you. With blue
brilliant eyes. And tucked
in pudgy hands, a yellow cup.

Right in the road.
You held out your calloused hand.
She took it, too. Just
going for a walk across
the yard, familiar rocks.
To chicken, biscuit smell. You knocked
the wobbly screen, gut
rumbling. Then: a silhouette
of woman wrapped in apron,
fisting a rag. Halved by newsprint,
a man sat behind her,
little boy on the floor
scattering trucks, a couch
sprawling out you wanted to slouch

your bones into. Instead: *Is this your little
girl?*" Back inside your rig moments
later, it was okay they didn't ask
you in to eat. You saw the woman's face,
how lost she was, remembering how futile
all her stirring, how quiet it had been,
the calling out of names: *Wash up, now!*
You left her in an O of thought, sifting
all she hadn't done, like sand, like flour.
Now, your engine smooths the gaps between
the unexpected. And when you're home, you'll flip
your hat aside, grab your glowing wife
around her waist, kiss her till she loosens,
recalls how close she was to dropping life
to ditch, to dust up like a yellow cup.

Mom & Tom Selleck

We all knew about him—even Dad, Man
of the House, Man of Demands—
but never why. At ten, how could I?
Hairy Mustache, Hairy Brows,
Hairy Hairy Chest Man?

At forty-three: I concede!
Conceive   the legs   (legs!)
the deep   deep dimples—no,
      mirth crevasses

and every girl he collects,   every cracked
      porcelain girl whose hair he strokes,
listening—   he is soft, not softened
by her, he is butter
      for every eggshell girl, butter that lives
on the counter, butter waiting for the cake . . .

(I know what you're thinking, and you're right)
yes, he holds them
carries their secrets
      like their bodies, like the snorkeling woman
facedown, with the animal print ass
yes she is faceless in the water

and he is grinning, he knows we know
      he is a boy, caught before he got the cookie
      and what would he do,
were we not watching?
      would he unzip like a wetsuit

and climb out hairy and Greek god stiff,
        what   is he waiting for
us to turn away?

No   this nymph has turned over, given herself
        over to him
a boy with knowledge, a body running on boyness,
                his hands
        just hands,   heedful,
not angry   not righteous

while she   floats   in muted light
        where goatfish schools prone
to rest are opening   making for her
        a gateway—   oh Mom,   meet Him
in paradise   that stopover on the way to Japan
        to meet your parents   and you
are young again   a hundred pounds lighter
        he will meet you   in his Ferrari, take you
                for a swim   take you to the tidal pools
bodiless,   you will be all arms and legs
        together you will
                stroke, stroke

'72 Datsun

In the blue cool of morning, before the reds
    had dressed themselves, we sipped our Yoo-hoos,

cocooned in blankets you'd tucked around us,
    blinked out the gas station glare and waited,

half-hidden in the back seat of that old gray car
    while you fetched your stack of papers.

Later years, and braver, we'd drop rocks
    down the hole in the gear stick's rubber neck,

watch the salt & pepper pavement blur to barcode,
    not quite all the way to gray, the way memory will.

Trash-can colored and rusty, it was a car all throat,
    all fits and stutters, a guttural language

choked at every breakneck shift of gears,
    a devil's-in-hell kind of loud, so buzz-saw loud

you could feel the fuel catch fire inside it, its inner life burning
    with something I was too small to name.

I wouldn't have known you were capable of past tense,
    of knowing things other than how to flick the wrist,

to clear your wobbly arm through the window,
    toss the newspaper to the sweet spot in the driveway,

or what else your mind might have been on
      as you made those stops by muscle memory,

what roads you might have taken, returning
      instead, every morning, to scrub

the soot of newsprint from your hands,
      only that we knew well every pause, every back

and forth, every house and turn of that route,
      that we were inured to that car's ungodly noise,

its roar turned cradle, learned what a body
      can shut out, and find itself rocked to sleep.

Self-portrait as Sinkhole III

—for Doris

I return to *Winterwood Lane,* named like a trickle
down the sweaty neck of a warm autumn, its trees
camel-necked, osteoporotic,

loose and leaning, an arm wriggled from its sling.
One, soldered at both ends to the ground,
its back arched with an old desire,

will never feel an ocean in its knees.
Counting the years since she last asked
is there a gap in the back of my hair

(it was white as spun sugar)
is a shrinking arithmetic—
ten, twenty collapse in the immediate air,

my thoughts stretch out like a hand
for nostalgia's loose change, some clue of her
my adult self might now decipher, some absolution:

no granny, I won't let them veil your face.
The house the neighbors built, dwarfed now
by shaggy silverthorn, bears one white square of paper

in its window, warning: Sinkhole, aft. Will any minute
collapse. And in its belly, metal chairs, broken bottles,
the night offerings of teens baiting nature, uprooting

whole systems of belief—*what is the seismic cause
for all that gives way beneath us—mothers
in their beds, frail as bird bones, cousins*

drowned, uncles, wood-stemmed, still whittling away . . .
The yellow tongues of live oak leaves
rattle out their shell speak as if they could say.

Post-hysterectomy Dream, 1959

You slip through my arms
like a bar of soap, a slick colt
just burst from her mother
still membraned, a yolk

tumbles over the shell, you fall
into fire and flame up,
shrivel to a raisin
i pull you out, whole and plump

now you are dirty, you need a bath
where is a basin
where is a bowl
where is the water to clean my baby

you are asleep on a slab
of marble, a stone cherub
where is a towel
where is a blanket for my baby

outside, a lake in the road,
there is mama and papa
there is your dad
here is our baby, my baby

where is the boat to get across
how will i swim and hold you

i will sink in the water and choke
how can i leave you

i won't
i won't

Study in Dread

How does a skull not cave like an eggshell
from the concrete block?

How does a man shake it off
and keep on going?

How does a body uncrumple itself
from the hatchback crushed by the backhoe, and walk

four miles to the hospital
with a broken neck?

What stops the man with canyons in his voice,
whose shadow eclipses that landscape

of rock, hard labor and fists,
who clawed his way out of the Great Depression

with the back end of a hammer?
We wait for him, hours gone,

to return and teach us a lesson
with that switch he'd sworn to cut from the woods,

the kind with the sapling whistle,
its own hoarse threat,

wait while the Highway to Heaven blurs
to local news, the voices barked and tinny,

while outside the shadows spread like a stain,
the strain on granny's eyes enough to light

the lamps. She warms the biscuits and the beans,
fills our bellies, willing him to hear

how locust-like the live oaks, how languid
the air, thick as drink, until the spent lilies wilt

like his urgency, conjure our blanched faces,
our smooth, inviolate hands.

Resurrection Body

Young, she was the platinum blonde
staring from the photograph, sepia landscape
fueling the heat shimmering around her,
her clothes—shorts? bathing suit?—rendered
by years and the faults of memory, irrelevant.
Only her body, posed on a blanket, matters:
one lean leg supine and white, the other
cocked, propping up the elbow, the hand
cupping the chin, the lips, the marvelous
white cheekbones, her marble
ripening to skin like Galatea,
her body glowing. Moon-white.

And when she gets it back:
will this be the body she wants?
The one smooth as mythology, before
it was flagged, pockmarked with debris,
barcoded with men's feet, before its sinkholes
yawned open, before its furrows plowed,
before its muscles learned to remember song,
or how to let go, before it became an archive,
evidence of all the bodies she has given
and received, before it was known,
and men could only howl up at that metaphor
for what shines in the dark?

A moment of silence

please, to honor our dearly departed
dinner, this slick pink mess which was once

a chicken. Let us honor what skill was lost
with granny, who could clean and cleave

the whole bird, could butcher with the best.
And let us mourn the passing of that word's meaning:

the fumbled punchline, the aria off-key, these
insult the butcher, who, prophet-like, can part

the fascial sheath, the silver skin like ribbon;
divine invisible lines of Hereford, of sea bass,

culling shapes, naming—the loin,
the sirloin flap, the clod heart. Can pop

the socket, peel the keel, avoid the coracoid—
oh priestess! Approach the infinite!

Divide, divide, divide!
You are never left with nothing.

What deer see:

the denim legs of a novice hunter
the cloudless sky, godlike, almost a future

green, in thickets,
the air foggy with green

the tremors of leaves in the air,
or back door snapping shut like a twig

at night, your car a bright blur
until it snaps into focus

and what she was seeing
with that extra layer of eye

shining back at you: more light,
a peephole into that other world,

that daughter universe
where the fractals of all your possible selves

branch out forever, and she stops to wonder
which one you will choose

At the funeral of a semi-distant relative

I am thinking of my own father
at the end of the pew, his hair
a great white ocean wave,
like winter itself. When the wind blows,

it lifts like a great wing, and flattens
when he sleeps, into cirrus clouds,
the view he sees looking into
his past. When we ask,

he pauses each time to see
if something will surface
like a dorsal fin, a fluke,
some sea spray hint of animal life,

then grins— *Three weeks*
is about all my memory is good for.
And I wonder which memories I'll cling to
and which I'll let go of when he's gone,

why his absence might somehow
make it easier to choose—as if letting go
is a matter of will power
when the memories cling to you

like burrs. I want to say I will miss
my father the way, in winter, you miss
the warmth of the sun
until you are stifling in August's

thick cotton. Is it love to worship
what someone never was, to burnish
their soot back to silver, like Aunt Blanche's
best tureen, it's bowl reflecting

some image of yourself you wouldn't mind
inheriting? Is there some nagging part of him
that knows the hours he's spent
tending every twig of the family tree

may not offset his younger self—
the explosions of ceramic, the sudden
absences, the air for days
serrated with ice?

If only the days we adored him
could claim us with the same
blue intensity: hot afternoons
at the weedy racquetball court,

and cool gas-station slushies.
Windswept motorcycle rides,
clinging to his back. Wrestling matches
on the living room floor. The nights

he'd invite us all to lie there in the dark
and watch the thunderstorm,
to stare down the face of our fear
and name it, find that counting out

its beats was a familiar kind
of survival, that so much panoply
was merely a matter of music,
of distance, a way to learn

what resurrection must look like,
how lightning's bright erasures
can bring you to the brink, and allow you,
again and again, to start over.

derrick

"Sometimes I wished to express my sensations in my own mode . . . ."

—Mary Shelley, *Frankenstein*

Cotyledon

To kill the time before dinner
instead of them
I drag my kids to the park

and watch them from a bench
do what kids do: run,
the only way to live

in the body, green their knees,
stare, brazen-eyed, graze
on the words of other

children, none strange (a word
only for adults) their truth
still chartreuse and capital.

They climb, get stuck,
the rite of unsticking
somehow, belongs only to

the first unsticker, the one
whose birth canal
they first burst through: you.

But mostly, I try to read
a book, recall how language
once lived in me, too

seedlings of vines
reaching up for sunlight
through my throat

it closes
thick, on *knucklebone,*
on *stone*

how many doors away am I
from that goddess
with the birthing tongue

I once spoke things into being
I once could listen
the trees are hissing, full

of insect wings in the dusk—
a crack, a glass shattering like a voice

I know—my boy

has tripped   *she made me chase her*
made me fall
O agony, O ancient Adam cursed,

here is my lap, let us sit
by the power derricks
chained to the horizon

let us listen
mommy, he says,
you can hear the wires crackle

Mommy Brain

What is the best trope

                mommy did you know vampire bats are real vampires

for the smell of her hair

                           Apple boss! Apple boss!

sweet smell of her skin

why does thought need

                                Mommy he called me a weirdo!

to be a train

               they turn into vampires they bite an animal and eat its

                 blood

barreling, one track

                             He said he never wants to hug or

                                 kiss me

only changeable

with a switch

                        Tease! Tease!

               and it takes an hour to eat it all and if they don't they

                  die and they fly

oh to have tracks

be grounded somewhere

                      faster than all the birds in the world

But could it be a boat,

                   Pop caw! Pop caw!

floating on a current

                         and he's mean to me all the time

but lilting, a yard northward
        and there's a brown recluse spider that's in Georgia and
      it can kill you!

will take it up the coast
        Knack? Knack?
or to south, farther out
to where the word ocean becomes
                I just love you more than the
                stars
another it's called
metaphor for the deep
      and what does a tarantula do

can swallow you up if you
           Mommy I want to talk to you, but just I
            don't know what to say!
find yourself
chasing a whale, can carry you

      and there's a goliath spider, i don't know what it does

to a place your hands will scar
          More! More!
and you forget
          you're the sweetest mommy ever
what has saved you

Father Tongue

—*after Stephen Dunn*

I've had to stop bowing down to that old
desire—a hand on the head in blessing.
Any string of words that might have meant
you are my pearl. Sure, I've accepted

pretty things: one sapphire pendant. A ring.
If I wear them from that prongy need, or some
frugality inherited like ear shape,
or a dextrous tongue—I can't say.

Is there any sugar I could speak
to loose the red drawstring of that face
so what emerges might be light-filled,
not merely facetious? What crystal might I taste

to unstone language, to make words
a matter of sticks to gather up and burn?

Self-portrait as Sinkhole IV

You will know me by my arm bone,
the one they count, the capital I
that says I existed.
Seventy-five hundred years
and I am not yet gone.
Near the burned rock middens,
a dead tree marks the ossuary.
Clamber down with your gift.
Comb the cobble, sift the chert
the shatter of flint, the sooty loam.
Set aside the crania
of vole, coyote, broken bear
mandibles. But the bangle
from a badger leg, the beads
made from rabbit bone, end
to end, notice: they were once
strung together, in a pouch.
Here. I was. I am. Count
the Harris lines. Like a tree,
I too have rings, a lexicon
to read: that I ate *lechuguilla*,
acorns. Not much *javelina*.
There was drought when I was seven;
prickly pear and opossum fed us.
Once, my father swapped his bear claw,
glossy slice of night, for a turtle carapace
from the Apalachee, carved from it a hair clasp.
Here it is, still cupping my head.
Please, resurrect

more than grave goods,
more than a conclusion: *death*
creates a hole into which
the social order caves, a new
direction for eternity.
That we had a faith, not
the weight of absolution, but
the wide tent of each other.

Eve in the Garden

Adam's in the field again, scattering leaves,
hoping for a crop. Twigs didn't work.
Just poked their heads ramrod straight
all day. He envied them their stiff inertia,
backs so straight, like God's bark

from the East. He doesn't know
she visits every afternoon, sneaking back
to gather green, tongue another taste, be filled again
herself, her melon belly sponge epiphany,
soak up the fecund air—and never grate his beard

against his brother. And every day,
she flits past the burning
like a moth, a hair for every visit
tipped in lightning, each white shaft
a thread of infinity.

Full

Before the fist in your belly tightens,
pulls you from your deep blue sleep,
plucks the strings of your hunger,
a minor chord echoing down the hall—
I feel the burn of your need:

milk-hard breasts, wheelbarrows
heavy with river rock.
This is the weight of mercy,
the body's need to empty itself,
to fill another.
(How could the bowel compare?)

And as you drink deep, gasping,
our skin thins to veil, our cells
translate a tongue we
don't need to understand,
your tongue, lapping, tells me
what you need, my body answers.
The truest kind of prayer:
the mouth, the open throat.

Feedings

"Her milk tells the baby about the world its mother has lived in." —Katie Hinde, Center for Evolution and Medicine

—for A.

Taste, daughter,
my story, before

language, before
the tongue acquires

its own volition, translate
my life to lipids,

my pain to fleshy thighs.
Tell me: what is the flavor

of endurance, the milk
of muscled will,

of backbending to your father?
Is the wine of compliance

red or white? How dry
is the vintage of these lean years?

Is there any fruit
of letting go, something

ambrosial, something
close to hope?

You will need something
let there be something

to fine the bouquet,
to fill in the hole

in my own father's heart,
let the tannins of that death

die off let this decanting take away
that blue swirl of ache,

the aftertaste of those years
I couldn't talk to God,

that vortex of buzzards
above the forest.

Prepare yourself
for what is not acquirable—

the briary, the thorn in the taste
of fatherlessness.

Ferber Method

Set your timer. Enter
your mind palace,
any temporary task

to distract you
from the breaking glass,
the chandeliers

fracturing to shrapnel,
breathing in
a cold and spiky effort.

Tell yourself this will do
no harm. No—less harm
than a mother in traffic bed heavy

or 3 a.m. angry that sacrifice
after all, is umbilical.
Ponder the liquid states

of the matter beneath you,
which is no sign of natural
disaster moving through you

snapping the oldest oaks,
all your inner orchards
uprooted like elephant bones.

You are not holding a live wire,
its current not turning
your inner workings to ash.

Pat him. Say *there, there.*
Make sounds with your mouth
he cannot comprehend

except to smell you,
to know you are there,
and not there.

Inure him to doubt,
the distance from him to summer,
its vines honeying the air

from some unspecified fence,
bragging its nectar
with little yellow tongues.

Portrait of Boy, Post-meltdown

You are retreating to indigo   *my edge of blue, my ultra-violet,*
devolving down to   *first cell of myself, my own start*

your dog particle—think thimble   *think the smallest of small spots*
think the moth mistaken for eyes   *too shivery to open*

I hold a ringful of copper things   *here I am at the vault*
needing you to speak   *hem-hawing*

but which will let me in? If there is *any tongue in which to say*
a lexicon inside you   *my brainbox is un-bricked is*

manacled, a language   *bean-cracked, de-forged, un-scrimmed*
afraid of liberation   *let us*

then trim language back   return to *yes* and *no,*
return syntax back to the body,   a thin finger of movement:

like that day, mid-September: the damp that clung all summer
to the skirts of the air at last   let go.

Found

tinker toy soldier star
two popcorn kernels salute
lego lego lincoln log
coin crayon torso blue

sock chalk puzzle piece
dandelion purple zoo
magnet strawberry carpet scab
limp lame lime balloon

ems and ems and ems and ems
candy wrapper candy-less
orange cracker crumbs go fish
cards jar Barbie dress

button block Hot Wheels car
dried noodle fetal curled
sock spinner thingy pink
Pop sickle stick—God

make this poem more than mess
but less pedestrian than this
carpet's sharp imprint—poor
instep, Lego-bricked martyr

when i was a cloud

—for Lydia, age three

and the sky was not   was never   was all sibilance and zither

    a fluency blue blue   sun imbued   I was the lucent

guess of myself   a plenitude less bodied less gaveled

    all morning and first   song all wing and priory

the feather's   clerestory   nothing yet to defy   before

    the tongue's kick   its glottal stop   all vowels

and ahs   I lived   where meaning lives   the throat's

    chancel   all desire was   my churning   my dirtied

feet   they purred   parabola'd to you   before I became

    the apple weight   thud in your lap   gravity's

little pink lady

What the deer remembers

when the bracken shakes first human
first chartreuse of any year all the lives
of the plowed earth the dream
of potatoes that sustains the waif
through the siege the long wait
in the ground for resurrection
forgiveness the vined and mossy walls
of the monastery the answer
to the question you don't yet know
how to ask the weed sprung up overnight
veins full of milk its leaves like fingers gripping
the bedsheet of earth moved with the fear
(like you my son) it may not be loved
so it morphs to seed becomes the first last
ubiquitous every possible future gowned in the air
a kind of knowledge like moonlight, its ache
its arcing voice and when I buckle
let me smell all this, your hair,
let it be the earth and hold me up

Red Crayon on Paper, 2021

Her baby finger blossoms
the page, poppies unfolding

their tongues, their little roars
of origins, of all the bright

insides of us, the heart's
plump apple bulb,

its contained little shuddering
fruiting the body, ballooning it

past its own orbit, the way a rusty
planet is a theory of salvation,

one cardinal a theory of awe
or a bright cherry bead

a theory of your mother
how the flock of them clicked

in your baby mouth
as you sat in her lap, content,

fat with her scent. To know then,
her body, that first room, first surety

of place, would be to return,
to know it close to death, flushed

with brushstrokes, its canyon
a flame of sunrise—but oh! to be

again, tucked tight to her chest
still clotted with cream and strawberry.

Combing My Daughter's Hair

Once, I pictured us in pinks and browns,
a placid-faced and rosy ritual.

Now I stumble through this riotous mass,
its expletives, its broken glass, made

> *mother   teeth   wolf   red*
> *wolf is howling in my head*

when I neglect the very thing you rage
against. Little one, this kind of start

must mean the end will be no tragedy,
the only wish I wish for you. Surely

> *comb   teeth   mouth   eat*
> *you would eat me like a meat*

somewhere in this thicket is a ram—
and can there be a goddess without loss?

Love, there is a grammar school for beauty.
How else could we understand, or envy

> *chop   toe   heel   shoe*
> *a pair of coal-hot shoes for you*

one another? And oh, to be envied!
The secret tarnished wish of any woman's

heart. Could I give to you, if not
with some aplomb or artful fairy thumbs,

> *heart   heart   liver   box*
> *stop the box me with your axe*

some kin to happiness—the enviable tress,
the bone-blessed magic comb—make you the future

subject-object of any tongue, grant you,
if not bewitching power to stop, to dumb it—

> *tongue   tail   knife   knife*
> *cut my tongue   to make a wife*

then, instead, a mother who could learn
the syntax of this tumbleweed, believe

whatever moves unrooted things. The way
they pink the desert's bright and boundless face.

sometimes I am surprised by my own placidity

—for Mila, my first

my girl comes to me, cowed, wide-
eyed with memory—a shoestorm,
sudden hot squall, sky-blackened

winds and debris, one purple tent
forever wrecked—pulls me to her room
mommy don't be mad to confess:

thick slick of ointment caked
on her dress, on all four walls,
the sheen of grease making

a maze of mirror mirrors—tell me,
who will be the victim
of this small crime?

> *Look— a grazing cow, her jaw pondering*
> *mysteries—nothing keeps the grass*
> *from worshipping the wind*
>
> *hold you, it was never about you*
> *let us lie down in this new pasture, sprawl*
> *in the soft grasses of some bigger love than us*
>
> *lose ourselves in their shush and sway, let cloud shadows*
> *wash over us, bless us with flickering light*
> *with miles and orchards of light*

Tail Elegy

Turbulence troubles the drain pipe, like fear's quick wings
in the belly—a fence swift, the same I'd freed weeks before
from his Rubbermaid chamber, his stump now
absolute, ghost limb of an old soldier, finding ways

to bear his ghost pain. He'd hobbled out, lingered there by the gate,
cowed like a man in a cheap suit, mustering dreams
of volition, pondering his state, how he got there,
so unprepared for the kids armed with crickets,

and worse—curiosity. How eager they were for the ambush,
the flick of his tongue's snap back like a carpenter's tape,
making the case for premeditation, evil's clean seed pit, soon
they said, imagining speech bubbles, whole narratives, whole

theaters of feeling, ordaining each other lizard bard,
lizard diviner, skink sibyl, the glass eyeball of future
still murky. The truth is: he never performed,
never confirmed one of their dreams, their interest withered

like a spent balloon, was mourned less. And when he hobbles away,
such evident wreckage—I will absolve, will let them forget
their tethering (to ourselves, to our God), that could we escape,
would be another kind of loss. Children, let us burrow together

into the neck of nature, believe every wounded thing
can summon a theory of green, some idea of itself,
and start over.

Rapture

They pinch flowers, hunt
sticks with knobby femur
ends, chicken bones
for spoons, a soup of dead
leaves and dirt, discover
a slick muscle carrying
a bone swirl, a helmet, snail
she tries the wet sound
in her mouth, watches it glide
up the post on a current
of light. She smells the tang
of loam, big world made of
old things, feels its whorl,
its aegis, its reliquary
of secrets, and before her
questions can thicken
into thought it drops
to the pavement, brother
tests the force of his baby
foot, feels the crunch
of an egg, an abacus bead,
surrender of sponge, leans
over to learn what wet shape
his power can take. And after
she has stiffened her arms,
wailing, after she has deflated
she turns her bright face up
talks about Jesus,
how he came back—
then curls her hands

into a prayer and watches,
waiting for that slug
to move. And before
I can find the words for what
an eon is, how to let her
down easy, how to believe
in something you only keep
in a closet to lug down
and dust off after funerals,
she has climbed out of that
abyss, her knees rusty
with clay, and run off,
one muscle of present tense,
her hair carrying
the light.

Eve at 87

—after Toni Morrison's "Eve Remembering"

I remember still the reedy ache
like the saxophone's need
swelling the tiled underground
inside me—Again! I'd say
if you asked. To swallow every seed,
to know the juice of anything!
That story? Like an old billboard, its words
now bleached to papery skin in need of sloughing—
Oh, what I know of God is not without the gavel,
not merely its wooden crack—but what I know
of the hand—the slick meat swell of lambing,
pink of my own cheek in the worm's
wet body, the pine's promiscuity in spring
chartreusing the world, the aspen's bony fractals
lacing the face of the mountain, autumn
strumming its amber ballads, summer
fields frothing with milkweed, the old girls
shaking out their hair, the ocean white
with miles of herring milt and egg, seagull clamor
hovering over glittering backs of their parents,
the hunger in every gelded landscape—
oh infinitely more! Could you dream what is past
the carnival of temporary outbuildings, the trailers
of belief, what lush grasses await, what whispers
there, what other prayers you haven't yet
mouthed, even for the grip of shards, a hard snow—
you too could bloom past a theory of fruit.
What is one paper bag's quarrel with the wind
against the river's muscling, its endless desire,
when every mouthless vine that seeks the light

is a prayer, when even the vulture
wearing her blackened grief
redeems the armadillo?

Something I Can Do For You

Nurses slam into gurneys.
Pills sprinkle the air. Red Jello Rorschachs stain the walls,
outside a lady and her dog are tangled in the trees, the leash
gone limp, in kitchens everywhere, cooks have lopped off fingers,
the sous chefs swim in a sea of metal, pots and pans chiming
their confusion and in some hotel, a pair of lovers thinks
they've reached some out of body free-fall, and they splash,
tractor trailers grind and twist on the highway in some slow angle,
cars thrust forward, drivers pump their brakes, splay their hands,
their noses against the glass to see
the whole world floating,
some apocalypse.

Tell me how long to leave them hanging there.
(I know this much: they must relearn their bodies.
How to maneuver. What is up or down.)
And when you're ready,
just before the atmosphere has burned away,
just before that last desperate gasp for air,
we'll let the earth start back its turning,
let them all drop in a dusty heap,
thud to their knees in strange backyards,
plunk deep into ocean, sinking with brick feet,
skid down some dotted desert road,
spine on bony spine.

We'll give instructions:
Stand, bruised.
Brush off the dirt and walk the long way back

to what you were doing.
You'll have time to think of it again.
Carry your broken thermometers,
your bent whisks.
Don't ask why, just walk.
If it's hot, strip off your sweater.
Wipe the sweat from your forehead.
Bear the sear of blisters starting at your heels
because your shoes aren't right for this.

Notes

"Motherhood as Safety Coffin": Emily Cook Dyches died in 2016 after suffering severe and ongoing postpartum depression after the birth of her fifth child. Her story has been shared by her family, who have dubbed similar maternal mental health challenges "The Emily Effect," hoping to raise awareness about the problems of post-partum depression. More information can be found at THEEMILYEFFECT.ORG.

Thanks

In the almost twelve years it's taken for this collection to take shape and find a publisher, I have had countless mentors and supporters I must sincerely thank.

First, my husband Rommel, who has generously said yes to every workshop and conference I've participated in through the years, despite the costs—of which my absence (when he re-learns our three children's demands) is likely the greatest.

My son, for whom apologies are more appropriate, for every night he's cried himself to sleep in my absence (despite his father's best efforts), who I hope one day will understand the need that drives a mother to exist separately— that often only distance can help one see beauty in the chaos of raising children.

My two daughters, also apologies for making public the tender and private moments of your lives, a privilege for which the window is rapidly closing.

My sister, who embodies a grace I aspire to, and who has been unfailingly supportive.

My mother, who has become my most reliable source of encouragement and validation, and from whom I inherited my love of the arts; and my father, for not disowning me as I make bare my perspective of our fraught relationship, whose life has arced towards love and forgiveness, whose every choice for the greater good I respect and am deeply grateful for.

I express heartfelt thanks for the nearly twelve years of excellent advice and encouragement provided by Steven Shields and Michael Diebert, as well as the many gallons of gas they've sacrificed to accommodate my attendance at our meetups, even after I moved to the suburbs. Their influence in these years has truly helped me hone my craft, and I'm confident these poems wouldn't exist without them both.

For Terresa Wellborn, Elizabeth Pinborough, Kathryn Knight Sonntag, Darlene Young, and Dayna Patterson, and all the opportunities you gave me to shape these poems—and to be seen.

For Julia Caroline Knowlton, whose early insights and validation helped me shape the collection. For Katie Chaple's monthly workshop, and our group of kind and honest readers: Karen Paul Holmes, Tim Payne, Sally Mohney, Trish Percival, Cynde Gregory, Skanda Prasad Ponnathpur Nagendra, Brooke Sparks, and Jane Simpson.

For all those who have encouraged me to not give up on this book, particularly at the Longleaf Writers Conference (which I highly recommend! Seth Brady Tucker and Matt Bondurant provide an incomparable experience.) I can trace a direct line from the events of that conference to this book award. I'd like to thank for Adam Vines for indulging my interruption to his dinner and sincerely providing advice about how to start this collection, as well as profuse thanks to Derrick Harriell, for his generous time and keen perspective that helped me envision this "body" in its final form. For their support, I thank Derek Otsuji, Laura-Joyce Hubbard, Chrissy Kolaya, Shellie Sims Welch, January Gill O'Neil, Tara Maher, Di Bae, and Lenore Mykah.

For Chelsea Rathburn and her generous encouragement of my work.

For Lynn Stowers and Donna Meredith, my former high school English teachers, whose early influences planted the seeds of a love of poetry (though they were admittedly dormant), and whose encouragement (and marketing efforts!) on my behalf have been a great blessing.

For Marty Williams, who was instrumental in pointing me towards modern poetry in grad school (before I knew I wanted to write), and whose support with my first chapbook was incredibly generous—a first collection wouldn't have felt possible without validation from someone I deeply respect.

For all of my *Segullah* sisters, who saw potential in my first attempts at publication years ago, who continue to provide a safe space for women's voices—and even a space to gather and encourage our inner artists: Linda Hoffman Kimball, Darlene Young, Heather Harris, Sharlee Glenn, Sandra Clark, Sherilyn Stevenson, Melissa Dalton-Bradford, Rosalyn Collings Eves, Melonie Cannon, Lara Yates Neidermeyer, Justine Dorton, Lisa Garfield, Melissa Walker, Emily Milner. And Angela Eschler, for pointing me to them in the first place!

For the Georgia Poetry Society, for providing opportunities over the years for me to meet fellow writers, read my work, and learn from more established writers.

For Elizabeth Gilbert, whom I have never met in person (nor virtually), but whose curated wisdom in *Big Magic* was instrumental, after having my third child, in recovering my voice and belief in myself—in finding time and space to create again.

Acknowledgements

Many thanks to the journals in which these poems first appeared:

491 Magazine: "Leaving California," August 2012.
Anti-Heroin Chic: "At the funeral of a semi-distant relative," October 2022.
Artemis Journal: "Feedings," 2022.
The Banyan Review: "Tail Elegy," Winner of the 2022 Banyan Poetry Prize.
Blue Lake Review: "Looking for the Soul Bone," March 2012.
CALYX: " '72 Datsun," February 2023.
Dialogist: "Mommy Brain," January 2021.
Drunk Monkeys: "Cotyledon," July 2022.
Halfway Down the Stairs: "Self-portrait as Sinkhole II," formerly "Self-portrait as Sinkhole," December 2022.
Irreantum: "Eve in the Garden," Summer 2011 and "Somewhere in this pile," formerly "Adjusting," Fall 2010. Reprinted in *Fire in the Pasture: 21st Century Mormon Poets. 2nd ed.* Summer 2011.
Literary Mama: "when i was a cloud," Fall 2022.
The Lumiere Review: "self portrait as ghost," October 2022.
Mom Egg Review: "What to Expect When You're Expecting," March 2017, and "Red Crayon on Paper, 2021," June 2023.
Orchards Poetry Journal: "Combing my daughter's hair" and "Father Tongue," Winter 2022.
Pilgrimage Magazine: "Study in Dread," September 2023.
Psaltery & Lyre: "Resurrection Body," May 2018.
The Resurrectionist: "Watermelon in Sapphics," formerly "Watermelon," June 2012.
Second Chance Review: "Rapture," April 2021.
Segullah Literary Journal: "Full," August 2018, and "When she wakes, rigid," January 2017.
Seven Hills Review: "Dad Feels Like Daniel Boone Inside," Penumbra Contest Winner, 2014.
SoFloPoJo: "Self-portrait as Sinkhole IV," formerly "Sample from Bering Sinkhole," August 2021.
Stirring: A Literary Collection: "Ad for Salems, 1978," Summer 2023.
Sunstone Magazine: "Motherhood as Safety Coffin," Spring 2023.
Susurrus: "What the deer remembers," Summer 2021.
SWWIM: "A moment of silence," February 2022.

Thuya Poetry Review: "Mom & Tom Selleck," Fall 2021.

Tinderbox Poetry Journal: "Ferber Method," December 2022. Finalist for the Brett Elizabeth Jenkins Award.

Trouvaille Review: "What deer see," July 2021.

Wayfare: "Eve at 87," December 2022.

WordCity Literary Journal: "Event Horizon," formerly "Inheritance" and "sometimes i am surprised by my own placidity," July 2022.

Yellow Chair Review: "Something I Can Do For You," formerly titled "What I will now do for you," February 2016. "Rock the Chair" Winner.

Young Ravens Literary Review: "Post-hysterectomy Dream, 1959," Winter 2022.